Testament

Sharon Sullivan

Copyright 2012 Sharon Sullivan

All rights reserved.

I have done my best to properly attribute any sources. The Biblical quotations are from the New American translation of the Bible, but I removed the verse numbers for a smoother flow.

ISBN-13: 978-0615658391 (Sunny Girl Press)

ISBN-10: 0615658393

Published by Sunny Girl Press

Dedication

This book is dedicated to the holy women of my Christian Life Communities small group, Renton Spirit Walkers.

Contents

About the Word and Words	1
Questions	13
What Church Means to Me and Why I'm Still Catholic	21
Keeping a Journal	39
Growing Up	49
Living Healed and The SPA Treatment	63
Priorities	89
The Presence of God	97
Water	105

Foreword

This is the first time I have included reflections that were not poems in one of my books. This book is mostly a reflection on my life and on what I believe, so I would call it my witness, or testimony. I am a poet who reflects on my experience of God. I have a Master of Arts in Transforming Spirituality (with concentration in spiritual direction) from Seattle University, which truly was a transformative experience for me, but it is nothing, means nothing, if I do not give my testimony. For those who are not familiar with the process of spiritual direction, it is a process of deep listening and prayer with the goal of helping the one who receives the direction to discern the best path to spiritual growth.

Acknowledgements

I could not have finished this project as well or as quickly without the help of my dear friend Liz Tidyman and my daughter Christine Ayala, who both proofread the book so lovingly, and the *Tuesdays with Deborah – Authentic Writing Provokes* writer's support group, who supported me through the process of online publishing. I also want to thank two women who have been faithful listeners, Cindy Rose and Sue Ferguson-Johnson. There are many more throughout my life who have inspired and encouraged my writing. Thank you. May God bless you.

About the Word and Words

And so we begin at the beginning:

Word

*Your Word creates light;
fills my soul's night with brilliance.
Your Word bears your spirit
into the depths of my heart;
transports me beyond the possible;
Your Word revealed;
the Word of the living God.
I tremble before your majesty;
I surrender my life to your love
for your Word is love;
your Word is life.*

The Word

*Spoken in the darkness;
spoken out of Love.
The Word
thundered without sound;
shattered the darkness with light;
illumined the world with Love.
The Word
Jesus.*

Song of Life

*In the beginning was the Word,
surely sung,
God's song of life,
song of love,
song of joy,
as God ended the silence forever.*

*Surely the universe resounded
with this music,
dancing into being;
sun and moon,
earth and water,
plants and animals,
dancing into life.*

*Who sings it now?
Who sings for the poor?
Who sings for the oppressed?
Who sings for the ones without hope,
unless we take up the song;
the song of life,
the song of love,
the song of joy...*

Surprise!

*They catch me by surprise;
those small events, or sights, or turns
of phrase that make me catch my breath
in wonder and delight. They tantalize my
senses; fill my mind with sparkling images
of unimagined possibilities;
and then the poetry,
the lush metaphors,
the thundering,
whispering,
singing,
words
flow
out.*

Ah!

Words

*These gifts
from unknown ancestors
have power
to move our hearts
to joy,
to grief,
to shame,
to jubilation.*

*Would we
recognize the feelings
if we could not name them?*

*Thoughts, memories
would-be images;
visions we could not share without…
Words:
bringers of companions
even in solitude.*

Nude in Black and White

With every word I write
I strip away the seals
that guard the inner linings of my soul.
My dreams walk naked in the light
for all who care to read.

A nude in black and white,
as slowly I reveal my secret meditations
with stroke of pen.

Yesterday's Songs

*Photographs;
visions of a youthful me;
pieces of my past,
they comfort me.*

*My poems;
Scraps of paper
squirreled away;
songs my heart heard
yesterday,
written down
with hope their spirit
would remain.*

*Such fragile things
are these
to hold my history;
to give me
an earthly
immortality.*

Our Song

*My prayer unfolds,
flowing from my heart
through my pencil.
And on a day of grace
we sing a song
of unearthly beauty;
a song with my words
and God's haunting melody.*

*We sing together,
God and I,
and dance
a poem of joy.*

*All of me,
all of me is
in the song;
all of me,
all of me
in the dance;
all of me,
all of me
in God.*

Praying the Song

*Words,
ideas,
longings,
praise,
seething inside me,
crying for release.*

*Music:
tone on tone,
melody on melody,
piercing me,
penetrating me,
splitting me open to Love;*

*music:
bonding to my
words,
ideas,
longings,
praise,
releasing them,
and sending them soaring
to You.*

Questions

Questions:
Science, Religion, and Poetry

How did science and religion get so opposed to each other? They ask the same questions in the beginning, and though I have to admit they come up with different answers, those answers are not incompatible with each other to my way of thinking. Moreover, those answers lead to more and more questions in both cases.

The methods used are, at least on the surface, quite different. Science uses the scientific method of experimenting until all the wrong answers are ruled out and one answer seems to work. Then this answer becomes a fact or scientific 'law' – that is until it doesn't work with a new discovery (ask a quantum physicist about this).

Religion uses stories of past experiences with that which transcends what we can see and touch (God). There is something in us human beings that recognizes the idea that there must be something beyond what we can experience with our senses, and it could be said that the very fact that we have this idea is proof that there is something.

The stories build up over the years and begin to have a congruence that flies in the face of coincidence. The stories are not called facts. They are called truth. Truth is greater, much greater, than the sum of the facts; at least this has been the case so far in my life experience.

There are scientific fundamentalists as well as religious fundamentalists, and they have a lot in common. They simply refuse to see that there is more. There is more than the Bible, and there is more than science and mathematics. Some say that humans invented God; I say that humans *experience* God (experience something greater than themselves, even greater than the world), and then invent religions in order to express their experiences. For those who would deny the presence of God, I ask, "What about fractals? What about music?" and if that is not enough proof – what about love?

I ask my own questions with poetry. Somehow it unlocks my mind so that I can connect with the transcendent reality of that which I could never understand or even name and certainly could never explain. My poetry does not necessarily give me answers, but it gives me a direction. There is something pure, something honest, about poetry. Somehow cloaking the truth in simile and metaphor has the effect of opening it up and making it more transparent rather than less. All this – and it delights me so.

The Question

*Listless and contrary,
I asked,
"What if there were no God
no God in me;
no God in the universe."
Briefly...so briefly
I looked into the abyss of emptiness.
A universe without God?
Cold; the accidental stars
twinkle,
give light, heat
for no real purpose.
Earth,
coincidentally alive,
lavish with life with no reason
for being, spins
aimlessly through a universe
crowded with useless wonders.*

*But...
There is Love.
undeniably;
incredibly,
incongruously,
surprisingly,
there is Love.
Love is.
God is.*

Death and Transfiguration

*We have seen the worm
become a butterfly,
and a tiny seed
grow into redwood tree
or rose bush in full bloom.*

*How will I be,
the risen me?
not just spirit,
not without substance.
I will have my body,
transformed
from dust once more.*

*How will I be,
the risen me?
How lovely is a butterfly?
How fragrant is a rose?
How mighty is a redwood tree?*

Human

To be human;
to fear death;
to ask why;
to wonder how;
to ache for love;
to yearn to pour out love.

To be human;
to be aware of me;
to see the power of my will;
to say no;
to say yes;
to withold;
to pour out;
always wanting more.

To be human;
to wonder
where we began;
to look beyond
humanity
for something more,
someone more;
to ask where love began.

I Wonder Gazing At Stars

I wonder
gazing at stars,
who is gazing back.
who wonders, dreaming,
if I am here?
Who imagines what
I might resemble;
what I might wonder
gazing at stars?

I wonder,
gazing at stars,
could the ones I see
be as many as the atoms
in one cell
of my smallest eyelash?
How many would it take?
Does someone
on an atom in my eyelash
wonder what I wonder,
gazing at stars?

*What Church
Means for me
And
Why I'm Still Catholic*

I wasn't always Catholic. I grew up in the Presbyterian Church in Memphis, Tennessee where we attended Evergreen Presbyterian Church. I don't really know about Evergreen, but my parents, as steeped in the scripture as they were, were not fundamentalists – and they were quite definite about it. I grew up loving the Bible, but knowing that there are almost as many ways to interpret the Bible as there are people.

I liked Sunday school and I loved singing hymns, however I was less enthusiastic about sitting through a long sermon. As a Presbyterian, I developed a strong conscience and a well developed concept of stewardship. These are hallmarks of Presbyterian spirituality, after all. I was taught to pray in my own words every night and to seek God's will in all of my decisions.

Oddly enough, my journey into the Catholic Church began in the Girl Scouts. My Senior Scout troop was half Presbyterian (sponsored by the women of Idyllwild Presbyterian Church) and half Catholic (sponsored by the altar society of Immaculate Conception Church). How's that for ecumenical before we even knew the word? During the summer when I was fifteen (in 1958), we went to Mexico. What an adventure! Of course, all of the churches in Mexico that I saw were Catholic. When my friends went in to pray, so did I (after clipping a hankie to my head – back then women were supposed to have their heads covered in the Catholic Church). I felt a feeling of deep peace in those churches, and I was touched by the devotion of my friends. It wasn't even Sunday, but they stopped to pray. I am sure they went to Mass on Sunday, but I don't remember what the rest of us did. The shrine of Our Lady of Guadeloupe was another place where I was awed by the devotion I witnessed. People were actually walking on their knees across the courtyard! I had never seen such dramatic devotion.

Then, when I was 16, I was dating a Catholic boy, a boy I met through one of my Girl Scout friends. I thought I loved him, and he said he loved me, so I began taking private instruction in the Catholic Church, to my parents' dismay. They worried that I would forget how to consult my own conscience and think for myself, but I knew that a strong conscience was too ingrained in my spirituality to disappear, even though the Church did not seem to encourage Catholics to heed their own consciences at the time.

I tried to explain to my parents that most of the things I was being taught were the same things they had taught me, but what I couldn't articulate was how I felt about Holy Communion. When I learned about the Catholic belief in the real presence of Christ in the Eucharist, it was as if I had already believed it without knowing. But my parents became more and more set against my joining the Catholic Church, and I had never been rebellious – moreover, I sensed that it would be hurtful to them.

When I was 18 and beginning my sophomore year of college, I ended my relationship with my Catholic boyfriend. That was when the really tough discernment began. I knew I would never be Presbyterian again, but I did not want to hurt my parents. My room-mate was Episcopalian, and I began attending her church. I could see that it was very similar to the Catholic Church. Furthermore, my mother had attended an Episcopal school for 12 years, so my parents would approve (with relief) if I joined. But I wondered if it was what God wanted. I had sincerely been looking for God's will in all this, but it was not apparent to me, so I made a "deal" of sorts. I said to God that I wanted to do God's will, whatever that was, but that I could not wait any longer for Communion and community. I knew that the official theology of the Episcopalian Church about the Eucharist was not the same as in the Catholic Church, but my heart said that those theologians were just confused. My heart said that the

Episcopalian Church had the "real deal." So I pled my case with God thusly: I said that I needed Communion and community, **and** peace in my family – so I would join the Episcopalian Church. However, If God wanted me to be Catholic, I would be Catholic. I just needed for it to be clearly God's will before I would hurt my parents. I needed a sign of some sort. So I joined the Episcopalian Church, and I loved it. I was active in the campus group and participated in mid-week Communion as well as on Sunday. When I went home, Mama and I went to church together. We were all happy.

In my junior year, I met Sam Sullivan and fell in love. Yes, his name is Irish, but he was not Catholic. He claimed to be an agnostic, but I didn't believe he knew what he was talking about. We soon became engaged to be married, and my prayer life became devoutly and intensely focused on his conversion into recognizing the great love of God. I never talked to him about it or specified a religion in my prayers. I just prayed hard and lived my own belief. If he wanted to be with me on Sunday, well, he would just have to go to church.

The next year, Sam announced that he wanted to join the Episcopalian Church, and he began to meet with the priest to prepare for this. I asked him about his agnosticism, and he said that *since he had experienced my love for him, he had begun to believe in God.* Wow! I was speechless with joy and gratitude. But that was just the beginning. On Thanksgiving, when he had been preparing to join the Episcopalian Church for two months, Sam said to me that the Episcopalian priest had suggested that he should be taking instruction in the Roman Catholic Church instead. I thought, "Huh?" And then Sam said, "I really think that he is right. I think I need to take instruction in the Catholic Church." My jaw agape, I said, "But, uh, but what about all those rules and stuff?" He said, "I know. I'll just have to take it one step at a time." And then I knew. I literally looked at the light bulb in the lamp over my head and silently said "Eureka!" (Yes, I really thought the word 'eureka!') "This is it, God! This is your sign!" I then told Sam that I would be going to those instructions with him.

My husband Sam and I joined the Roman Catholic Church together three months before our wedding. It was 1964, and Vatican II was in progress. 1964 was the year in which the process of changing from Latin into English began. To say that we joined the Church in an exciting time would be an understatement.

A lot has happened since then, and I am still married to Sam, and I am still a practicing Catholic – with plenty of ups and downs in both relationships. I have my own tensions with the Church, but I know I'm not going anywhere else. I am a practicing Catholic. I like that word "practicing." It means more to me than just participating in the worship and practices of the Roman Catholic Church. It means that I am still "in training" as a Catholic Christian. I need lots of practice to get it right, as I practice for the big event when I go home to Jesus.

But the Church is a mess. It is full of sinners and people I have nothing else in common with. Well, of course it is a mess and full of sinners: it is comprised of human beings, and I am a sinner too! I have belonged to the Presbyterian Church, the Episcopal Church, and the Catholic Church, and I have visited numerous other churches. They too were comprised of humans and thus sinners, and all have plenty of messy problems which give their members "excuses" to opt out. If anyone thinks he or she can escape the messiness by finding a different church, I say, "Good luck! You'll need it!" I also would tell him or her that Christ was present for me in every one of these churches. None of us has the "only way" or even the "best way" of following Christ. We need to have a spirit of unity, a spirit of love, even in our differences.

Yes, I have belonged to a parish that was so torn by ethnic differences that no diocesan priest wanted to be the pastor there. This divisiveness developed after an era of cooperation and growth that was extremely exciting and promising. But there had been undercurrents, and the undercurrents took over. The parish is still there, and healing has taken place, but I mourn what it could have been.

Yes, I have been in a parish in which the parishioners became divided about their pastor. Former friends in bitter disagreement formed separate factions. It was a terrible upheaval that caused some to leave the parish and perhaps even the Church. The divisiveness broke or strained long-time friendships and finally forced the reassignment of the pastor. The parish found healing and has become stronger as a parish, I hope.

The early churches of Corinth and Ephesus (and others) had similar problems, to Paul's great exasperation, but somehow they stuck together and grew, as have we who remain Catholics today. Here we are, still Catholic in spite of the pedophilia scandal and other scandals; in spite of disagreements and factions; and in spite of occasional bad leadership. Here we are because we want to practice being Christians, and we can't really do that alone. Here we are because Jesus promised to be with us when we gather. It's a guarantee that I can sit next to Jesus for at least an hour a week, more if I want, and that I can hear his Word proclaimed. (I do realize that I can sit next to Jesus on the bus or in the park as well...)

I also get to express my gratitude and love through words and song - and then I even get to receive the presence of Christ physically into my own body at the Eucharist . I love the liturgy and the stately dance we call Mass. I love the songs and the way they mesh into the readings from God's Holy Word. I love the great poetry of the Gloria and the powerful words of the consecration. I love how we all make physical contact with each other as we say, "Peace be with you." I love looking at my brothers and sisters in Christ from my vantage point in the choir after Communion and thinking of the wonder of how we are all one body in Christ. Where else can I go for all this? All these wonderful experiences happen in community – where two or more are gathered in Jesus' name. I have to show up, at least. We all receive a blessing just for showing up. And we are called to carry that blessing out into the world along with the Good News. Let's not forget that! It is more important than all of our worship and prayers put together.

God knew that I would thrive spiritually in the Catholic Church. That is why God sent me here. I am glad that I was listening all those years ago, and I give thanks to God for this blessing in my life.

I find my parish community to be a dynamic and caring parish, though there are still plenty of tensions! Just bring up the subject of stained glass windows. However, we remain a spirit-filled community of love, a vibrant community of stewards – which means that we are committed to <u>more</u> than just showing up. But the first step <u>is</u> showing up – showing up <u>awake and listening</u>. Here I am, Lord, I come to do your will.

The center of our worship is the presence of Christ in the sacrament of the Eucharist, or Holy Communion. The Catholic Church teaches the theology of the real presence of Christ under the appearance of bread and wine. I cannot explain this mystery, and I think it is a mistake to try to explain how it is so, but we cannot resist.

What I believe is in my poems. Here it is in prose: We are, undeservedly and amazingly, called to be the incarnation of Christ in the world today. We receive this gift, this calling, through Baptism and through receiving the Holy Spirit, and we celebrate it in the Eucharist (which means thanksgiving). The Eucharist, or Holy Communion, is a physical sign of this spiritual/physical phenomenon. We physically receive Christ into our bodies to express our willingness to carry Christ into the world and our unity as one body in Christ, and, for me, the Roman Catholic Church expresses this as well as humans can.

While reflecting on church, I looked it up in the Encarta Dictionary, which is included in my word processing software (Microsoft Word).

> The first meaning given is that it is a building for public worship.
> The second meaning given is that it is a religion's followers as a group, or body of worshippers.

The Catechism of the Catholic Church says so much that I can't even give a proper synopsis here, but most often, it refers to the church as a group of believers – as the Body of Christ.

Then I looked up Catholic and catholic (capital "C," lower case "c") in the same dictionary and in the thesaurus, and found this:

Catholic (adjective)
Cath-o-lic (kathlik, kathalik)
1. **Roman Catholic**, belonging to or characteristic of the Roman Catholic Church
2. **Christian**, belonging to the community of all Christian churches
3. **of historical united church**, belonging to the united Christian church that existed before its separation into different churches, or to any church that regards itself as continuing the traditions of that united church

Cath-o-lic (noun)
    Church member
    A member of the Roman Catholic Church

cath-o-lic (adjective)

1. **all-inclusive**
including or concerned with all people
2. **useful to all**
useful or interesting to a wide range of people
3. **all embracing**
interested in or sympathetic to a wide range of things
Some synonyms for catholic in the thesaurus are: "wide-ranging, broad, all-embracing, extensive, and varied."

None of this surprised me. I knew the definition before I looked it up, but the thesaurus also gives an antonym, or opposite, for catholic. The **antonym** given is "conservative." CONSERVATIVE? This is the opposite of catholic? That did surprise me; not because it goes against the grain for me, but because it is not the opposite of what many want the Church to be. When I had finished laughing, I thought about the Holy Spirit (Yes, the Holy Spirit is in the Church, in the churches – in fact refuses to leave us alone!).

The Spirit is certainly not conservative; the Spirit is way beyond what we think of as liberal. The Spirit can't even be categorized, but the word *radical* comes to mind. All our ideas of order and harmony go out the window when the Spirit blows in. The Spirit has order and harmony all right – just not the kind we recognize. We think of order as organization, and we think of harmony as including peace and quiet. I don't dare to guess what the Spirit thinks. I just know that when you decide to let the Spirit fully take over your life, you'd better hold on to your hat! You are in for a wild ride!

I must add, however, that all our prayers, all our worship, all our church attendance, all our devotions (all my poems) mean nothing to Christ unless we are loving one another as he has loved us; that is his commandment. This sounds easy until we remember that this is not a sweet, feel-good kind of love. This is a sacrificial, let-yourself-be-crucified kind of love that is not just for our friends and families, but also for those who are alien to us and those who are our enemies.

My Catholic Questions:

Blessed Sacrament

Flat white wafer;
holy,
consecrated, suspended
in a starburst of gold
gathering the light
that plays
on the altar.
Where is its power?
How is this
God on earth?
If I broke the glass
and crushed the wafer,
would it cry out?
would it bleed?

Yet I find
at that moment of communion,
when I consume the wafer
with my sisters and brothers,
holy we...

here

is the power;

here

is God on earth.

Now he will cry out with our voice,
Now he will bleed with our blood,
Now the wafer - we,
are the very flesh;
the very blood
of Christ.

It Doesn't Make Sense

Bread;
not even bread as I know it,
but a thin white wafer
made of wheat;
stored in this fancy box we call
tabernacle;

"Are you in there, Jesus?
Many years ago, I know,
You called me here;
To this faith,
But it doesn't make sense now.
You said that sacrifices and offerings
Are nothing to you;
That following you is
Everything…
*But you **called** me **here**.*
It doesn't make sense."

"What?"

"I love you."

I heard you,
I heard you there,
in the tabernacle,
and that doesn't make sense either,
but now I don't care.
You don't have to make sense
when you are Love.

At the Foot of the Cross

*Here I am
at the foot of the cross,
a cross I imagine rough
and heavy with suffering;
dark and streaked with pain.
It was an instrument of torture
and a gift of love.
But I am here, open-eyed;
I am here, all of me;
here with all my wounds
and blessings;
with all my failures
and triumphs,
with all my faults
and virtues,
my memories of helpless rage
and my memories of love.
Here I am
at the foot of the cross,
looking into the face of
outrageous, foolish love.
Here,
today,
all of me,
I say Yes,
I will let myself be loved
with this
irresistible,
terrible,
magnificent love;
even though I know
it means I must learn
to love this way.
Here,
today,
at the foot of the cross,
nothing is impossible.*

Temple of the Spirit

Holy ground!
I take off my shoes
and gasp in wonder
at the presence of the Spirit
here in my body.

You fill the spaces between the atoms,
yes even between the atomic particles
that comprise the atoms of the cells
of my body.

How could I not sense it?
How could I not feel
the breath of your Spirit
filling me;
refreshing me;
renewing me
in this sacred embrace?

My whole being sings
with the transcendent joy,
the wonder,
of your presence
here
now
in me.

Mass on Vacation

*With sunburned noses
and wrinkled T-shirts;
redolent of cocoa butter tanning cream
and Deep-woods Off,
we gather as strangers
at an unfamiliar altar.
Strangers;
yet sisters and brothers –
Unfamiliar;
yet it feels like home.
Brought together for an hour,
we celebrate our union
as Body of Christ.
We are strangers,
yet we are one body.*

Asking for Grace

*Every time I talk to You
I am like a college student
calling home;
(except I ask for grace instead of money).*

*Please send more grace.
I need mercy, too.
Again.*

And you always send it.

*I need Your grace
To be who You want me to be.
I need Your grace
As I need air to breathe.*

The Meeting

*I bring my shell,
my "where I am;"
worries,
cares,
questions,
compulsions.
I lay them in your heart,
listening,
opening;
and I meet myself,
and You,
in my center.
You -
speaking in my voice
You -
whispering on the pages of my journal
You -
forming words, ideas, images in my heart
You -
being me;
me -
being you
in a moment of love-giving;
a lifetime
in a moment out of time.*

Keeping a Journal

All through my life I thought about the idea of writing poetry, books, or articles. I would read about authors and how they wrote, and often they would say that they wrote in a journal or diary, saying that this practice was a great help to writers. Some even said that it was essential to write in a journal. Even knowing this, I was never quite able to give myself to the routine of writing in a journal in my youth. Now I do not know whether I could function normally without it.

I communicate much more effectively on paper than I do face-to-face. Somehow, in a conversation, I often know I have an insight to add, but cannot formulate the words until the subject has been changed. I feel tongue-tied and inarticulate. I feel stifled, but it isn't anyone's fault. It's just my slow inner processor. It's as if I have a dial-up modem while the others have the latest high-speed cable. I am still pondering a subject that they were discussing thirty minutes ago.

When I was about forty, I did begin to write in a journal. I sometimes write daily, sometimes weekly or even less often, but I have continued the practice ever since. My journals contain prayers and my raw, unedited poems and the musings that led to them. They contain dreams that I just had to write down, as well as my questions and pleas to God. If anyone were to read my journals, she would know my heart, my struggles, my sadnesses and my joys. Yes, I have kept them because, when I go back and read old journals, I find poems and reflections I never finished. I also find prayers that have been answered; struggles which have been resolved.

Struggles:

Sin

*Hands on my ears
I chant,
"I can't hear you!
I can't see you!"
My eyes are closed
against the truth,
against the light.
Deaf and blind,
I stumble
and grope.
I stub my toe
and curse the rock.
Later,
in a moment of grace,
I find the rock
I cursed,
and it is my sister,
I see her,
bruised and resentful,
lift up her hands
to close her ears.
Her eyes are closing
against the light
against the truth.
She begins the chant,
"I can't hear you!
I can't see you!"*

Killing Time

*There is death in my life
where I hide from the light:
turning off my feelings;
tuning out the voices
that may cry out for help.
I beg for more time:
precious, priceless time.
"Where does it go," I cry
so innocently,
when, under the edge
of being aware,
I know,
I must know,
the murderer is within.
I have killed too much
of the time entrusted to me.
I spend it,
waste it,
kill it
with empty,
meaningless
pastimes.
Why?*

Desolation

*I saw my poems,
my banners of truth,
and was filled with disgust:
how awkward, how stupid, how jejune,
how unpoetic and trivial;
bits of trash, remnants of a
narcissistic frenzy of self-pity.
I was ashamed of them,
ashamed of needing help,
ashamed of my weakness,
my powerlessness.
Why am I ashamed of that
which gives me grace?
Something in me clings to
the darkness of power.
Something in me invests in evil.
God, get me out of this!*

Trials:

Holding Pattern

*Suspended above the fog
we circle
and circle again;
we seem to hang motionless.
Helplessly caught
between yesterday and tomorrow,
we float –
waiting for God
to tell us where home is,
or if.*

*Staring into
the nothingness
of not knowing,
wolves I've seen before
come prowling, howling
through my soul.*

*In both white-knuckled fists
I clutch my talismans,
my memories
of the ends of
other holding patterns
when the fog cleared,
and we, though tired
and bruised of heart,
found safe landing
and came home to love.*

Peeling the Onion

*I peel off false serenity
and find a cauldron of fury.
If I peel off the fury,
I find fear.
If I peel off the fears
I will find the heart of the onion;
I will find pain.
Here is the sobbing child
crying for Mommy.*

No wonder onions make me cry.

Tiger

There is a tiger in my heart,
tearing, rending, tattering hope;
leaving only

imagined scenes of loss
and darkness,

glimpses of a dark night of the soul
yet to come,

echoes of a requiem
yet to be written,

a chill of winter
in the midst of August.

Must I hunt this tiger?
May I simply set her free?

Growing Up

Growing up:

My parents were a beautiful couple when they were young. Actually, they never grew old; my mother died at age forty-nine, and my father was fifty-five when he died. They loved each other in spite of their faults, and they loved their children unconditionally. Our home was filled with books and music and also with family, friends, and Irish setters.

My parents had a strong faith in God, which they handed on to me. They prayed together every night before going to bed, even in the hard years.

They also handed on their values about the equality and dignity of each human person, loyalty to family, and care for the earth.

We were a magnet for kids because of all the above and the fact that my parents could be a lot of fun. But my father had a drinking problem that started small and grew into full-blown alcoholism by the time I was in my teens. I was the oldest of four girls, with a gap of six years between me and the next, so I was witness to the hardest years, those just before he went into treatment. Even after that, alcohol was a constant struggle for him, but he had AA, a family, and a job to keep him sober much of the time. It was only about a year, or even less, after my father went to AA when my grandmother offered to pay for my freshman year at any college away from Memphis. As my father said, the family dynamic was not good for me. No one talked about "co-dependency" back then, but my parents had realized that I needed to get out. My "exodus" was another priceless gift from my parents and my grandmother. When I succeeded at college beyond their expectations, my grandmother continued to pay for the next three years.

The next two poems are perfect examples of co-dependency

The Diplomat

*They call me peacemaker, diplomat
and put me right to work.
I speak Mama's words to Daddy
and I speak their words to my sisters.
I say (to myself) that I feel like
a ventriloquist's dummy, that I'm tired
of speaking other people's words,
but this is a lie.
I love the power, the
seductive, glamorous, captivating power
of their dependence on me.
So I let myself be a ventriloquist's dummy.
What are my words?
What does my voice sound like?*

Home for the Holidays

I'm home again, sucked in again,
trapped in the eddies of family;
trapped in the same old role:
arbitrator,
peacemaker,
go-between,
parent-daughter,
torn between pride and exasperation;
I still love them all.

But let's have fun!

The Indian:
A Ride to School

Our family car had two wheels
and a chief's head on the gas tank.
My friends with nice cars
stared with envy when
I arrived at school
on the back seat of the Indian
clutching Daddy's jacket,
my hair tucked in a scarf –
watch out for the exhaust pipe!
How they crowded around!

The Indian:
Turkey Chase

Jeans, boots, and jackets,
my hair tied in a scarf,
we ride an adventure
through the fields,
over log bridges,
into the forest
where no road goes.

Encapsulated in an aura
of flying thunder,
I cling to Daddy's jacket;
his body shelters me from the wind
as we fly on the flat and bounce on the rough.

Other cycles join us on this journey
– scary and comic by turn –
paladins questing for thrills
through ditches, in the mud
and sharing mud freely in spatters.
Finally, we laugh and shout as we relive
each bump at the end of the course.

Blackberry Joy

*Wild tangles of
brambles twist
a fierce
protective net of thorns
around their jewels,
lushly burdening every branch.
Deepest purple black
they shine
among the shadows;*

Blackberries,

*ripe,
bursting with
sweet and sticky juice,
challenging us
to venture forth
to compete with wasps,
braving the
vicious, tearing thorns,
we fill our pails
and emerge
wounded, juice-stained
warriors eager
to enjoy the spoils
of jam and cobbler.*

The Hi-Fi

*Christmas morning you surprised us all
with a gift that wasn't under the tree.
(Christmas was really one of your best times
until it became your best time to drink.)
It was a high fidelity record player
that played a new kind of record
with a new kind of sound... there were speakers
on the wall...your body vibrated with pride and excitement
as you showed us all the features, and then you put
the first new record on the Gerrard changer
and we heard JOY TO THE WORLD
so loud, so large we hurried to open the door so
the neighbors could listen to the rich,
enormous sound of Christmas
while we danced around the room singing with it.*

The Glance

*On an Ozark afternoon in June,
the sun squeezes perfume from the cedars
as we gather there, ten teenage girls
trailed by assorted parents –
just here for the ride – and to keep us out of trouble.
But I see you have a pint of gin, Daddy,
tucked away in the trunk.
As you reach down
to take a swig, you glance at me
as if I were a co-conspirator,
as if you thought it might be ok with me.
Or perhaps it is a glance of apology; still,
it is a glance I cannot meet lest I turn to stone
just as Midas' daughter turned to gold at his touch.
Did you think I gave permission?
Did you think I understood?
Did you think no one else would notice?
Did you think of me at all?*

For my parents:

Young Mama

When I was very small,
and frightened by
the secret shadows of the night,
I knew a conquering sorceress,
filled with loving Mother's Might.
She filled my dusky room
And all the corners of my life with light.
She cast a magic spell that sent
my monsters into flight,
and then she kissed my sleepy eyes good night!

Mama

Ahhhh,
Mama!
stretched on the cross
of family,
a cross stained with tears of rage,
but a cross
endured with love.
You loved me.
Did you forgive me?
I just assumed – I never really knew.
Did you let the pain go?
I never felt it go.
Did I beg forgiveness?
How could I be forgiven
for following Jesus?
Could I?
Could you?

Heirlooms

*Family heirlooms; ageless antiques
passed down from generation
to generation:*

*anger
bitterness
violence
addictions*

and

*love
tolerance
wonder
faith.*

*How do they come together in me?
How do I destroy them?
How do I preserve them?
How do I transform them?
How will I pass them on?*

To My Parents

*You've been gone so long,
yet present in my life;
you live on in me;
With my sisters
I am what is left of you
in this world today.
But it seems an empty presence
when I want to hold your hands
or hear your voices
or laugh with you, and see
my life reflected in your eyes.
No, I cannot have this
no matter how I yearn.
I miss you.
I will always miss you.*

*Who remembers now
my first step,
my baby talk,
my toddler giggles?
Who can tell me
stories of my childhood,
ones I was too young
to remember?
It seems as though that part
of me died with you,
just as part of you
lives on in me.*

*Living Healed
And
The SPA Treatment*

Living Healed

Don't we all want to be healed of something? It could be a disability, or illness, or pain; or it could be a crippling lifestyle that has become an illness, such as alcoholism, overeating, or addiction to something else. It is a place of darkness in a life that yearns for light.

So what holds us back? Do we believe we deserve our illness? Do we think we should just take what life brings and make the best of it? Do we believe that God wants us to suffer, is punishing us? Do we believe that miracles* don't happen any more – if they ever did – and that "faith healing" is fake? Are we afraid of how life will be without the illness?

Sometimes our "unwholeness" is not something we can control by lifestyle, and we have tried prayer and laying on of hands with at least the faith of a mustard seed, yet still we are not healed. I cannot explain why this happens. I know people who have been healed through prayer, and I know some who have not. But even if we are not healed, we can do our best to live as if we were healed. What does this look like? It looks like the paraplegic who plays wheelchair basketball and does community service projects. It looks like the kid without arms or legs who has learned to do ordinary tasks without them and goes around giving motivational talks. Their dark places have become beacons of light. We do not have to be defined by our disabilities. We do not have to lie down and quit living a full life. We do need to turn to Christ for healing and light with a willingness to go where he calls us to go. Only then can we be whole.

*Let us remember that miracles can (and do) come about through natural phenomena as well as through what we cannot explain naturally.

The SPA Treatment (since we were speaking of healing)

Some years ago, in October, my daughter and her fifteen-year-old son moved away to Phoenix. Besides being my daughter, she is my best friend, and I grieved her absence. On top of that I had been spending my weekday afternoons taking my grandson to gymnastics, driver's ed., and wherever else he needed to go.

Their absence left a great emptiness in my life, and I came to realize that I had ordered my life around them. My afternoons now yawned empty. During November and December I was busy, but after the holidays, I had plenty of time to brood, and I became "stuck."

I spent January and half of February doing as little as possible. The regular things on my calendar were kept, but I made no medical appointments even though they were due. I did no exercising and very little praying and writing. The house was messy. Things my daughter had left here were still sitting right where she had left them in October. I just ate, played computer games, and read novels. I was in what I call a 'blue funk'. Then one day, as I prepared to meet with my spiritual director, I wrote in my journal:

> I am not in a good place. I hope and pray that today I will talk about what I really need to talk about instead of finding diversions. I am in transition – seemingly stuck in transition – and I tend to bury the part of me that is kicking and screaming while I pretend that everything is ok. But I sit at the computer too much. I do not take time apart every day or any days to pray unless I am preparing for Bible study or my prayer group. I do not pray the Examen prayer. I am not exercising. I eat too much. I am not adding any ministry to fill the void. Nothing. And I have plenty of time.

I wanted to pull out of this. I wanted to be healed. Then I wrote:
> I <u>could</u> volunteer at Pregnancy Aid, St. Vincent De Paul, a local bookstore, etc… But that would mean making a commitment. Am I ready for that?
> Should I make a decision when I am like this, or is a decision what I need to get me out of it?" I made a list of things that help keep me close to 'the tracks'.

Then I met with my spiritual director, who encouraged me to make a decision even if it was not the very best one. I began making decisions about my daily life, and I chose writing as my main ministry.

Then I wrote in my journal:
> Moving toward a better place:
>
> Structure   \
> Prayer   My SPA retreat in
>   everyday life
> Action   /
>
> It's a SPA treatment. I have an acronym!! <I was chuckling – then I continued> Why did I make this acronym, SPA? It just sort of happened in my writing. Perhaps I wrote it because an acronym gives structure. It is also a memory booster."

Then I did what I always do when I am beginning a new spiritual journey. I got out a new journal, the fanciest one I had. It had been a Christmas gift; the pages were edged with gold, and it had this quotation engraved on its cover of creamy white leather, "…If you can believe, all things are possible to him who believeth." Mark 9:23.

That day I downloaded some poetry by Rumi onto my iPod nano and listened to the poetry while I went for a walk (action). I took time from my day for prayer. I included a sort of Examen, but without all five steps. The steps vary, but roughly they are: 1. expressing an awareness of the presence of God, 2. an expression of gratitude, 3. going over the previous day and identifying those times of living in the light, 4. identifying those times when I stepped into the darkness, and 5. making a strategy for the new day which will lead to light. I was skipping the first two steps, but it was some structure.

The next few days I introduced the structure of weighing myself and testing my blood glucose every morning. I also began writing something for my book (the one you are reading) every day. After three days, I found that I was becoming bored by computer games. I reveled in listening to Rumi's poetry while I walked, and I began making a "to do" list each morning. I made an appointment for a medical check-up. Also, I signed up for a Conscious Dreamwork workshop at a nearby priory and for Catholic Advocacy Day at our state capitol. These things seem so small as to be trivial, but they had a profound effect on my well-being. I told my small sharing group at Bible study about my SPA treatment, and they said it was brilliant. One of them suggested a website called "flylady."
I told my spiritual director what I was doing, and we rejoiced together, but she suggested that I take all five steps of the Examen prayer. I began using all five steps the next day, and I was visiting the flylady website daily too. Bit by bit, the website got me started on the house. Before I knew it I was into spring cleaning in spite of a nasty cold. My SPA treatment was just the jolt I needed! Then when I told my friends how I was getting along and what I was doing, I was surprised to find that they thought a SPA treatment like mine was what they needed in their lives too. That is when I decided to write about it. But SPA can be different for different people. Each person needs structure in her own way (or his own way). The same goes for prayer and action.

Structure:
Every life needs structure. It is especially helpful in times of great stress. In fact, if you look at your life, you will find structure there, even if it is in the midst of chaos. However, when we are in a time of stress or when we are seemingly stuck in the wrong pattern, it is time to revamp.

Start with a few simple changes. Look at your morning routine and your bedtime routine. Have a routine. Make lists. Try flylady.com.

Prayer:
Set aside a time dedicated to prayer or meditation every day. Have a specific place for it; a specific time is also a good idea. Write in a prayer journal.

Action:
Start a new project. Exercise daily. Do something creative every day. If it is Spring, start a garden or at least plant something and take care of it. Write about your progress.

I hope the SPA treatment is as healing for you as it was (is) for me.

The Seeping Wound

*I believed I could put the past away
like old worn-out stained towels
and start over with new feelings,
new relationships,
but what are these stains, these
blotches of pain?
I sealed it in. I did. I sealed
away the pain, the anger, the fear.
No;
No.
Now I see.
My heart is like a wounded
finger, bandaged over but still seeping,
soaking the bandages and
making bloody prints on
everything I touch.*

Ambush

*Seeking healing,
my wound is an opening
to my inner life, inviting
all sorts of visitors.*

*I yearn for the ocean,
but the healing beach is hidden
behind a veil of cloud and rain.*

*I am surrounded by companions.
Cocktail party laughter whirls around
like snowflakes in a blizzard.*

*One fleeting giggle attacks my heart
in an ambush of memories,
dreams, and desires;*

*and at the punch line,
instead of laughing,
I choke on my tears.*

Spring Garden

*I brought myself,
still stiff and sore at heart
from the wounds of winter,
to the unturned,
weedy garden soil;
digging,
throwing weeds aside;
throwing grief with them
where soft spring sunlight
warmed the just-turned soil,
filling the air with
the dark mysterious scent
of life that was
and life as yet to be.*

*Spring sunlight
lay gentle on my back,
loosening my muscles,
unclenching my heart,
inviting me to sing
for the simple joy
of being
Alive.*

Subversive Love

*Just when I think
I'm lost,
abandoned,
shivering alone at
the brink of the abyss,
I discover
I'm found*

*flying with angels,
soaring among stars.*

*YHWH,
you turn my life
downside-up-inside-out.*

*You heal my wounds into
blessings.
You transform
my failures into
grace,*

*grace that washes
my heart
with an everlasting
baptismal
rain of love.*

The Blessing Year

*Seeds of hope,
planted in the soul's
dark night,
germinate in the soil
of failure and confusion.
The first shoots emerge
in a barren field,
chilled by the winds
of early Spring.
Wait...
Labor...
Endure...
The time of toil
and anguish will pass.
Then will come
the blessing year;
a year of bountiful harvest
with love and grace
so succulent
the joy runs down my chin.
Partaking,
I become the harvest.
Joy and love burst
from my every pore.
I can feed multitudes
with such
bountiful fruit*

Coming Home

*I come to the ocean,
and somehow it feels like
coming home.
I never lived near an ocean –
What is it?*

*Rhythmically pounding waves,
the cleansing tides,
rushing winds bearing
the tangy taste of salt -
and something more –
(it tastes and smells alive).*

*Do these evoke primitive memories,
memories without words
or pictures to organize
them in my mind,
memories of my beginnings
in my mother's womb?*

*I feel connected
to the rhythm of
her beating heart,
the rushing wind of her breath,
the tides of her digestion,
the tangy, salty taste and smell
of body fluids – life-blood.*

*I feel connected.
I feel at home,
wrapped in the memory
of my mother's womb.*

The Touch

*The touch of God;
so new, so fresh;
like a babe
still wet from the womb;
or a new-born galaxy,
expanding across the sky.*

*The touch of God;
so deep, so strong;
to be described
in words
not yet spoken.*

*The touch of God;
so swift, so sudden;
the mind cannot keep pace
with the joy.*

*The touch of God
turns a life like a page,
changing it for all time.*

More Poems

Fireworks at an Ocean Beach

*A hundred bonfires
splash pools of golden light on
the vast darkness of the beach,
their windblown, spiraling sparks
dimmed by a kaleidoscope
of jeweled lightning bursts
- fireworks -
erupting everywhere in a
bedlam of light and color and
crackling, banging sound accompanied
by the constant rhythm of the booming surf
and the whipping whoosh of the wind.
I breathe the air
.....smoke, sulfur and salt.....
and laugh;
one side hot to the fire,
one side cold to the wind,
and even after half a century
of fireworks displays,
something young and untamed
inside my middle-aged, settled
self responds to the wild
chaos of color, light, wind, surf and flame
with a child's delight,
excitement and wonder.*

Exploring Creeks

*I remember exploring the creeks
of my childhood;
stair steps of multicolored shale
marked with prints of beings
of another age,
rippled
with sun-starred water
marbled
with shifting leaf shadows,
the rocks
moss-slick cool and wet
on my dirty sweaty feet as I hike
ever higher and deeper into
the wilderness,
seeking
the source.*

Burning Bush

*Standing barefoot
in the sacred, freezing mud,
I listen for the voice of God,
for I know you are here.
I hear your whisper
Piercing,
blowing everywhere
through the trees, all ablaze
with the unconsuming fire
of autumn.
You tell me to rejoice
in the coming winter;
love the wind, the cold,
the death,
for the journey through death
will bring new life.*

Autumn Leaves

*Sometimes I almost weep
in wonder watching leaves
gather golden light into
themselves until they seem
to glow with their own light,
filling a gray autumn day with joy
in the light before winter.*

*Sometimes I almost weep
with grief as I see
my knobby knuckles
bespeckled with blotches of brown,
my sagging skin and graying hair.
I look away and feel
the chilling fear of death
or disability.*

*Perhaps God
sees other marks of age:
my heart polished smooth and bright
like a shining river stone,
my soul sculpted by suffering
for those I love,
my mind fully ripened by wisdom
learned through the years.
Are these my autumn leaves,
heart-stoppingly glorious and bright
in the light before winter?*

Winter Rain

*Soft, the silver sky
reaches in drifting mists
to touch the earth;
trees stand motionless
in silent meditation,
drinking in the quiet, cold
winter rain.*

*Soaked spongy turf
squishes underfoot.
It has drunk its fill,
and still the rain
slowly seeps down
filling the ground
with tiny river systems
to reflect the silver sky.*

*This is a time for quiet hearts;
for pausing to listen
and remember.
It is a time for pondering
the mystery.*

Winter Sunlight

*On a day of bitter cold,
the dry snow squeaking
underneath my booted feet,
the winter sun surprised me
with its blinding brilliance on the snow;
a brilliance giving no warmth
to the body, but it burned in my soul
as I walked,
my nose hairs stiff with frost.
And then...
surprise!
Appearing and disappearing as
suddenly as falling stars,
ice crystals danced in air,
transformed by the sun into
tiny diamonds flashing
rainbows
in the winter light.*

Christmas Cactus

*In the dark days just before winter
the Christmas cactus on my window ledge
bursts into bloom,
dripping with flowers of pink and white;
sexy little things
with stamens and pistils
thrust outward in wanton invitation
for a consummation that will not
come in captivity.
I feel a pang for such
unrequited lust that ends
with wilted blossoms
littering the counter
like tiny, bright, empty condoms
unrolled, but never used.*

The Day After Christmas

*Open boxes
and rumpled papers strewn
where the pregnant presents lay
'til yesterday;
yesterday, when we
held our breath as we watched
with hope that our gifts
would bring delight and joy
to those we love.*

*Promises fulfilled,
the empty boxes remind me
that the waiting is over,
has been over
for 2,000 years.
Christ is with us,
And in us,
eagerly anticipating
as he watches with hope
that his gift will be received
with our delight and joy.*

Today

*Today…
a once-in-a-lifetime event;
never seen before,
never will be seen again.*

*Today…
an opportunity to be
the person
I aspire to be.*

*Today…
endless possibilities
present themselves
like flowers to be admired
or gathered.*

*Today…
could be my last chance
to watch the sun rise,
hear a child's laugh,
smell a flower,
touch a kitten,
or look into your eyes.*

*Today…
what a marvelous gift!*

The Dawn

At last!
The dawn;
that breathless pause
between the darkness and the day.
The edge of night
begins to glow;
an opal mist
with flashing hints
of rose and blue,
and those who sleep
begin to wake
and fill their throats
with songs of praise.

At last!
The dawn;
death transformed to life.
I'll rise to meet the light
and join the song
with alleluias in my heart
for golden clouds
and diamonds at my feet:
for light that fills my soul
with joy.

At last!
The dawn.

Priorities

"Where does Christ fit in my life?" is not the right question. The real question is, "Does Christ live in me and I in him?" If Christ lives in me, then Christ is the center of my life, not just first; Christ is the beginning and the end and the center. With Love as the center, I can't go wrong.

When I do go wrong, it is because I put fear in the center: fear of death, fear of failure, fear of poverty, fear of abandonment. Like Peter on the water, I look away from Christ, and I sink in the waves. However, even then I am not lost if I cry out to the Lord, return my focus to Christ and accept his helping hand of grace.

It seems to me that all sins are based in fear. Greed comes out of fear of not having enough. Hatred is bred by fear that "the other" will hurt us, or fear that "the other" will hurt us again. We can't forgive because we fear that "the other" does not deserve it, as if any of us deserve forgiveness. Pride is born of fear that we are not good enough and fear of failure. Sexual sins are born of fear that we will not be loved, fear of abandonment.

Each of us has a "root sin," something that we struggle with all our lives. My "root sin," laziness, causes me to stray from following the path God has chosen for me. Actually, in truth, my root sin causes me to sit beside the path. I haven't strayed away, I just am doing nothing but look at the path and daydream about it, or worse, I am simply doing nothing at all. My priority has to be to act, to do something in order to focus on God, so I write my prayers in my journal, thus combining an action with prayer. I institute my SPA treatment. This is not the answer for everyone. Some folks are _too_ busy. They need to stop doing and practice being. Centering prayer would, perhaps, be a good antidote. We each have to figure out our own way.

Multiplication of the loaves

*It is enough
to be just one
sourdough starter;*

*enough to raise
a whole batch of dough;*

*enough to be a miracle for
countless loaves
year after year,*

*giving my all to each loaf
for a joyous expansion of life,*

*trusting that each time
I will be renewed
in the giving.*

My Desire

Yahweh
I yearn
to return your love;
each breath
a breath of desire for you;
a holy sigh of love
that gives me life;
each word
a song of longing for you;
an endless song of love.
I lean toward you
like a plant leans toward the light.
I search for you
as the river searches for the sea.
Yahweh,
you are
my breath
my song
my light
my life.

Nothing is Impossible

With God
nothing is Impossible:
the building destroyed
is whole;
has not yet been built.
The ones we lost in death
are found;
are, this very minute,
conceived
in the wet heat of love.
Mary is saying yes;
Jesus is crying out
his agony on the cross
and is putting Thomas'
hand into his wounds.
And, yes, I am young
even as my hair silvers.
With God, it is all
happening today,
right now,
this very minute.

The Locked Room
John 20:19-23

Sometimes,
like the disciples,
I lock myself into
a room;
a room of fear,
a room without windows.
I convince myself
the locks will keep me safe,
as if I had not brought
my confusion and fear
into the room with me.
But when I look,
suddenly
here you are,
filling the room
with love and peace
until the very air I breathe
is you.

This came from my dream of an old woman and a small boy by a lake.

Transforming Spirituality

*Old Woman,
Old Woman,
would you be new?
Open your eyes
to the glory of dawn;
open the eyes of your heart
to the miracle of one drop of dew.*

*Seeker,
Seeker,
Would you be found?
Live side by side
with the homeless ones;
open your arms
to embrace the lost.*

*Little Boy,
Little Boy,
would you be blue?
Bathe yourself
in a stream of prayer;
immerse yourself
unceasingly in prayer.*

The Presence of God

The presence of God is manifested in the vastness of the universe, but also in the particulars; in the tiniest details. The presence of God is in every breath I take and in every beat of my heart; in the tiniest seed and in the patterns of the veins in a leaf. But am I paying attention? I cannot escape the presence of God, but I can, and frequently do, ignore it. Every once in a while, I am smacked in the face with breathless wonder. Sometimes I look at the stars, and it is as if I had never seen a star before, and I am overcome with the wonder of it. Last spring, when the first flowers opened, I was so delighted with them that I took photos of each new flower, zooming in close to get the tiniest detail. In those instances, it was easy for me to be aware of God's presence.

But everyday living has a way of distracting me from the wonder. This is easy; I just let the tasks and concerns of the day take over – or I focus on what I need to do tomorrow or the next week. I hurry from one thing to the next, leaving no time for quiet contemplation, no time to notice God's presence. Another way of saying this is that God is always present, but I am not always present. Then I need to work harder at awareness. Sometimes a whole day goes by, and I wonder what happened to the day. Where was I? Well, I wasn't fully present, that's for sure. Even more difficult are those times when everything seems to go wrong. The year after my daughter moved away, I was plagued with illness and troubled at heart. It was a great grace and blessing in my life that I had begun to work on attentiveness to the presence of God. Notice that I said attentiveness.

Attentiveness to the presence of God is seeing beyond the surface, seeing into the heart of a thing. It is listening into the silence or listening beyond the noise and finding God there; being present to God. Attentiveness to the presence of God takes some effort at first, but it can transform the way we see the world and the way we hear it. This does take vigilance, or watchfulness; but if this watchfulness is to take place all the time, it needs to be a watchfulness that continues in the background of other activities since we are not contemplative hermits, and we don't spend all day in contemplative prayer. We work, we shop, and we drive in traffic.

I have this little game I play while driving. It began as a car game for the family when travelling. Each yellow car or truck counted one point. VW bugs and Hummers also counted a point. Yellow Hummers and bugs counted double. Lately the kids have become tired of the game (well, they aren't kids any more either). Still, my awareness of yellow cars continues. Anyway, a while ago this question was given to me: "What can I do in my daily life to become more aware of God's loving presence in my life?" At the time I was spending a lot of time driving in heavy traffic, and it came to me that I could let the yellow cars be reminders. Every time I see a yellow car, I remember that God is here and loving me. I notice them even when I am talking or listening to music. Underneath whatever I am doing, I think "yellow car!" and simultaneously I think "I love you too." It feels like a lover's glance from across a crowded room.

This silly little car game has transformed my driving experience, but the awareness went beyond driving. Whatever exercise of attentiveness we practice in our lives has a way of expanding beyond itself. Now, I don't even have to see a yellow car, because I am looking for them. My awareness is in the looking. And I wanted to expand this awareness to the rest of my life, so I looked for other reminders. I did not find one that worked as well as the yellow cars, but looking for the reminders was enough to get me going. I was being attentive just by trying.

Being attentive to the presence of God is not enough by itself, however. We also need to let go of our own desires and pre-conceptions because they obscure God's desires for us.

Mist

Relentlessly present;
surrounding my life
without walls
you are here,
always
here,

but obscured
by the mist
of my own
desires and expectations
as I grope through
this rocky cliff-hung life.

How clearly I see
through someone else's mist
the way so bright,
so straight,
so smooth
in my eyes.

Sadly, for my own,
too often I have preferred
the mist
or denied its existence.

Still
You are here,
surrounding my life
without walls;
You are here,
always
here.

Today
I see You.
That is You, right?

Resurrection Day

Weary travelers, one day
We left our cares at home
And took a ferry ride to joy.
Sun-stars winked on the bay
Where whales played peek-a-boo.
We shared bread in the wind
With all who would partake.
We will never eat so well again,
For we who had been so dead within,
Were now alive and playing by the sea.
Life was everywhere:
Crabs and starfish in the tide-pools,
Clams squirting from their hidey-holes,
Seagulls soaring in the wind,
And life was in our laughter,
Our freedom,
Our joy.

Water

John 4.7-15

> A woman of Samaria came to draw water. Jesus said to her, "Give me a drink." His disciples had gone into the town to buy food. The Samaritan woman said to him, "How is it that you, a Jew, ask me, a Samaritan woman, for a drink?" (For Jews use nothing in common with Samaritans.) Jesus answered and said to her, "If you knew the gift of God, and who is saying to you, 'Give me a drink,' you would have asked him, and he would have given you living water." The woman said to him, "Sir, you do not even have a bucket, and the well is deep; where then can you get this living water? Are you greater than our father Jacob, who gave us this cistern and drank from it himself with his children and his flocks?" Jesus answered and said to her, "Everyone who drinks this water will be thirsty again, but whoever drinks the water I shall give will never thirst; the water I shall give will become in him a spring of water welling up to eternal life." The woman said to him, "Sir, give me this water, so that I may not be thirsty or have to keep coming here to draw water."

John 7.37-38

> On the last and greatest day of the feast, Jesus stood up and exclaimed, "Let anyone who thirsts come to me and drink, Whoever believes in me, as scripture says: 'Rivers of living water shall flow from within him.'"

I was a white girl growing up in the South in the 1940's and '50's. I attended segregated schools, rode in the front of the bus, and drank from the fountain with a sign that said, "Whites Only." From the sign, you might get the impression that there was something special about the water in that fountain with the sign that said, "Whites Only." And it *was* special. It was poisoned with hatred and fear; water without life.

My parents gave me something very different. This is what my parents taught me: God made human beings in all shapes, sizes, and colors. Each human being is different from every other human being, and each human being is precious in God's sight; no human is more valuable to God than any other. In fact, all of creation is valuable and precious in God's sight. And I thought, "Who am I to disagree with God? Why would I want to?"

My parents also taught: How boring this world would be if we were all alike! What would there be to learn about each other? And it doesn't matter that some of us are smarter or faster or stronger or more beautiful in the eyes of the world; we do not derive our value from our abilities, nor do we derive our value from what we look like. *God gives us our value by loving us into life.* Where did my parents get such wisdom in that culture; in *any* culture? I can only surmise that they had some of that living water to counteract the water without life; at least enough to <u>teach</u> the truth, if not enough to <u>live</u> the truth fully – like many of us. My parents knew the truth, but they did not want to experience the turmoil and trouble of the Civil Rights Movement. Some take a lifetime to begin. Living the truth is not easy; some never do. Some jump right in, but even then it takes time and work to really get to it. I try.

For example, I know that while we are all different, we are all valuable and precious in God's eyes. Not only do I believe it. I know it.
And yet…

And yet sometimes I still struggle with the fear of those who are not like me – those whose customs, beliefs, languages, manner of dress, or color are very different from my customs, beliefs, language, manner of dress, or color. I am unsure of how to converse with *them*; what I might say or do to offend. I don't know what *they* are thinking about me. What if *they* hate me? Yes, I am more likely to think *they* hate me than I am to think *they* love me. Do *they* wonder about the same things I wonder about? Of course *they* do. We all wonder why we are here, and we wonder how the universe works and why it works at all.

Unfortunately most of us believe that we have the best or the only answer.

Especially when it comes to politics and religion, it is tempting to think that *we* are right, and therefore *those people* are wrong. Even if we <u>are</u> "right," that "rightness" does not have to mean that those who disagree are evil, or even that we are better people than they are. Why do I struggle with this issue when I know better? Perhaps the whole problem is the word "they." The more I think of "them" as "us" the more I am able to lay down my fears and pick up love instead.

And this all sounds really wise and neatly concluded until…. Wait a minute! I can slide into this kind of thinking even while dealing with my own family members! Yikes! I need a drink! (of *living* water!)

Fountain of Love

YHWH,
you are a fountain of love
spilling over the universe,
watering us, loving us,
until we love;
until we become fountains.
You will never
give up,
even as the water of life
sinks into the dry sand
of our indifference,
and we cry out in thirst
as we clutch cups too full
of hate and greed to hold love.
Even now,
you will never
give up.
No word or deed is
praise or thanks enough
until I love:
until I am a fountain.

Water

*All the water on earth
has always been on earth
or in earth's atmosphere,
they say;
a circle of living water
giving life to the earth
and finding renewal in the sky.*

*Do I cool my feet in
water from Jacob's well?
Do I bathe in water that
baptized Jesus?
Do I drink a tear
that Mary wept
at the foot of the cross?*

Baptism and Grace

*Lost,
I embraced my death;
ice-bound in my frozen tomb;
tomb of anger,
tomb of bitterness and loathing,
tomb of dark-night.*

*Still,
I heard the faintest
distant whisper-sound;
a tiny ripple in the
hidden recollections
of my heart.
How could I hear it, I so dead,
so far from life?
Was it your voice?*

*Something
made me turn around...*

*You are here!
Holding me close
in the blazing,
sparkling light
with colors of joy
dancing all around.
You are here,
Baptizing me in my tears,
washing me alive again.*

www.ingramcontent.com/pod-product-compliance
Lightning Source LLC
Chambersburg PA
CBHW031405040426
42444CB00005B/423